1 9 8 6
The Year You Were Born

Birth Certificate

Name: _____

Birthdate: _____

Time: _____

Place of Birth: _____

Weight: _____ Length: _____

Mother's maiden name: _____

Father's name: _____

To Caroline and Kelly Martinet from Auntie Jeanne J.M.

To Bethie, Jill and Dara J.L.

1 9 8 6
The Year You Were Born

Compiled by

JEANNE MARTINET

Illustrated by

JUDY LANFREDI

Tambourine Books · New York

U.S. Almanac
1986

International Year of Peace

World population 4,938,000,000

United States population
241,596,000
Males 117,820,000
Females 123,776,000

Number of children ages 5 to 13
30,346,000

Number of births in the U.S. 3,757,000
Boys 1,925,000
Girls 1,832,000

Average length at birth 20 inches
Average weight at birth 7 pounds, 7 ounces

Day of the week most babies are born Tuesday

Deaths in the U.S. 2,105,000

Immigration to the U.S. in 1986
601,708

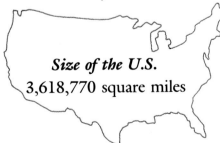

Size of the U.S.
3,618,770 square miles

President Ronald Reagan

Largest city
New York, population 7,236,000

Biggest state (in area)
Alaska, 591,004 square miles

Most rural state Vermont

Longest river Mississippi-Missouri, 3,710 miles

Tornadoes 764

Households with TV sets 85,900,000

Households with VCRs 31,000,000

**Average number of hours per week kids
ages 2 to 17 watch TV** 25

Top crop Corn

Total 1986 output 210,000,000 metric tons

Beverages consumed 136.6 gallons per person

Number of new cars manufactured
7,829,000

Children's books sold 237,000,000

Most popular musical instrument Piano

Boy Scouts 4,037,000

Girl Scouts 2,248,000

Favorite food
Hamburgers
(18,000,000,000 eaten in 1986)

Most popular ice-cream flavor
Vanilla

New patents (inventions)
76,000

January

January is named after Janus, the Roman god of doorways and of beginnings.

BIRTHSTONE *Garnet*

WEDNESDAY
January 1

New Year's Day • President Ronald Reagan and Soviet leader Mikhail Gorbachev exchange greetings on television; Reagan's message is broadcast in the USSR, and Gorbachev's message is broadcast in the U.S.

THURSDAY
January 2

In Boston, Massachusetts, the 52-story Prudential Building catches fire. The mayor rushes up 11 flights of stairs to help 2 elderly women to safety.

FRIDAY
January 3

EMERGENCY LANDING: A plane with an engine dangling loose makes a successful emergency landing in Dallas, Texas.

SATURDAY
January 4

Trivia Day • At dawn, the famous Nevado del Ruiz volcano rains sulfuric ash. This is its first activity since the eruption of November 13, 1985, which completely buried the town of Armero in Colombia.

SUNDAY
January 5

3 international art thieves are arrested as they are loading 2 wooden crates into getaway cars. The crates contain 105 ancient art objects worth a total of $18,500,000!

MONDAY
January 6

2,800 schoolteachers in Oakland, California, go on strike.

TUESDAY
January 7

In Seattle, Washington, state officials set off underwater firecrackers to scare away sea lions from a fish ladder at the Ballard Locks, where they are eating all the salmon and steelhead.

WEDNESDAY
January 8

NASA announces that the *Voyager 2* spacecraft has discovered a 6th moon orbiting Uranus. • In Oahu, Hawaii, 36 bodyboard riders from 6 countries compete in the Morey Boogie Bodyboard Professional Championship.

WHO ELSE WAS BORN IN JANUARY?
BENJAMIN FRANKLIN

U.S. statesman, diplomat, inventor, scientist, printer
He helped draft the Declaration of Independence.
BORN January 17, 1706, in Boston, Massachusetts

THURSDAY
January 9

U.S. and Australian researchers report the discovery of a substance called interferon alpha-2-B, which may be helpful in preventing the common cold.

FRIDAY
January 10

TOY SPREE: At 9:30 A.M. (PST), contest winner Tina Thompson, a 12-year-old from Sioux Falls, South Dakota, is given 5 minutes to take anything she wants from a giant toy store. Everything she grabs, she can keep!

SATURDAY
January 11

British explorers reach the South Pole on foot, after following the route of antarctic explorer Captain Robert F. Scott. A ship on its way to pick up the 3 explorers sinks in the Ross Sea.

SUNDAY
January 12

After being postponed a record 7 times, the space shuttle *Columbia* finally blasts off from Cape Canaveral, Florida. The crew carries lucky charms; one even wears a Groucho Marx mask.

FUN FACT '86

In January, the U.S. Postal Service reports that entertainer Bill Cosby receives 20,500 letters *every week*.

MONDAY
January 13

Astronauts aboard the *Columbia* zap 10 soap, shampoo, and toothpaste products with laser beams and cosmic radiation to test how well they would stand up to life in outer space.

BIRTHDAYS IN 1986

THE TUXEDO 100 Years!

THE AUTOMOBILE 100 Years!

ALUMINUM 100 Years!

LIFE MAGAZINE 50 Years!

Coca-Cola 100 Years!

THE STATUE OF LIBERTY 100 YEARS!

New York Public Library 75 Years!

PLEXIGLAS 50 years!

HARVARD UNIVERSITY 350 YEARS!

OREOS 75 Years!

THE SALVATION ARMY 100 YEARS!

THE DOUBLE-DECKER CHEESEBURGER 50 Years!

THE Peace Corps 25 Years!

THE San Francisco SYMPHONY 75 YEARS!

GODZILLA 30 Years!

HAWAIIAN PUNCH 50 years!

TUESDAY
January 14

Scientists announce that a sinkhole in Miami, Florida, has revealed surprising new evidence showing that human beings lived there 10,000 years ago.

WEDNESDAY
January 15

President Reagan's dog, Rex, returns to the White House after having his tonsils removed.

THURSDAY
January 16

In Washington, D.C., a bust of Martin Luther King, Jr., is unveiled at the Capitol Rotunda. • The pollen from cedar trees in San Antonio, Texas, is causing 50,000 runny noses!

FRIDAY
January 17

More than 200 of the country's top Scrabble players gather in Atlantic City, New Jersey, to compete in a Scrabble tournament. • Space shuttle *Columbia*'s landing is delayed because of rain and clouds.

SATURDAY
January 18

Pasquale "Pat" Consalvo of Staten Island, New York, wins a $30,000,000 lottery jackpot—the second-largest lottery prize ever won.

SUNDAY
January 19

A 4-foot-long boa constrictor is found at the St. Louis Zoo in Missouri: Someone brought it to the zoo and left it behind! • Ronald Tiekert wins the Scrabble tournament in Atlantic City, New Jersey.

MONDAY
January 20

The U.S. officially observes Martin Luther King Day. It's the first year the day is celebrated as a national holiday. • France and England announce plans to build a 31-mile tunnel under the English Channel.

TUESDAY
January 21

Hug Day • Concorde's 10th birthday: The special anniversary flight from London to New York takes only 3 hours, 22 minutes.

WEDNESDAY
January 22

WORLD'S COOLEST ART: Artists create 10-foot-high masterpieces out of snow at the U.S. Snow-sculpting Contest in Milwaukee, Wisconsin.

THURSDAY
January 23

National Handwriting Day • The price of oil drops to the lowest it has been in 6 years.

FRIDAY
January 24

Traveling at more than 45,000 miles per hour, U.S. spacecraft *Voyager 2* flies within 50,679 miles of Uranus—its closest approach—and sends back thousands of photographs of the planet.

SATURDAY
January 25

NASA scientists announce that *Voyager 2* has discovered another moon orbiting Uranus, making the total number of known moons 15. Only 5 had been found before the *Voyager 2* mission.

SUNDAY
January 26

Full Moon

The Chicago Bears defeat the New England Patriots, 46–10, in football's Super Bowl XX in New Orleans, Louisiana. 73,818 people attend the game, and 127,000,000 watch on TV!

VOYAGER II SIGHTS URANUS

Uranus is the 7th planet from the Sun and the 3rd largest of the solar system's 9 planets. It's 5 main moons are: Miranda, Ariel, Umbriel, Titania, and Oberon. Uranus, which is about 2 billion miles from earth, was first discovered in 1781 by William Herschel. Astronomers knew very little about this bluish-green planet until the U.S. Voyager 2 flew by it on January 24, 1986.

Uranus Fact File

Rotation period (length of day) • 17.2 hours
Atmosphere • 88% hydrogen/12% helium
Rings (made of large particles) • 10 major, 100 minor • Moons 15
Other features: 125 miles-per-hour winds and a strange emission called electroglow

MONDAY
January 27

BUGGING BUGS? Research scientists report that they have found a way to listen to insects eating, using high-tech surveillance techniques.

TUESDAY
January 28

In the worst disaster in the history of space exploration, the U.S. space shuttle *Challenger* explodes just 73 seconds after liftoff from Cape Canaveral, Florida.

WEDNESDAY
January 29

Paleontologists report the discovery of 200,000,000-year-old crocodile, fish, and dinosaur bones in Nova Scotia, Canada. Also found: the smallest dinosaur footprints anyone has ever seen!

THURSDAY
January 30

Police disarm a bomb found at a McDonald's restaurant in South Bend, Indiana.

FRIDAY
January 31

An earthquake shakes parts of Pennsylvania, West Virginia, Indiana, Illinois, Michigan, New York, and Wisconsin, and sets off alarms at a nuclear power plant near North Perry, Ohio.

BULL STAMPEDE IN TULSA, OKLAHOMA

BIBLE TRANSLATED INTO NAVAJO

BIOLOGISTS WITH NETS CAPTURE CONDOR

CHALLENGER SHUTTLE EXPLODES CREW DIES

February

*T*he name February comes from the Latin *februa*, which means "feast of purification."

SATURDAY
February 1

Restaurants, homes, and shops are flooded in Venice, Italy. 3 days of rain and high winds have caused the canals to rise more than 5 feet above normal.

SUNDAY
February 2

Groundhog Day • America's groundhogs predict an early spring—they don't see their shadows.

MONDAY
February 3

BACK TO SCHOOL: After almost a month, the teachers' strike ends in Oakland, California. • In Augusta, Georgia, a pilot lands a plane at the wrong airport!

TUESDAY
February 4

President Reagan delivers the State of the Union message to Congress. • The principal of an elementary school in Ossining, New York, has barred Garbage Pail Kids, the popular trading cards, from school.

WEDNESDAY
February 5

An antique teddy bear is sold in London, England, for the amazing sum of $3,837!

THURSDAY
February 6

Bus driver Vanessa Eaton leads 47 children to safety when her bus stalls on railroad tracks in Perry, Michigan.

FRIDAY
February 7

Jean-Claude Duvalier, wealthy dictator of Haiti, flees his country, along with his wife, children, and 20 other relatives.

SATURDAY
February 8

Debi Thomas becomes the first black skater to win the U.S. Figure Skating championship. • The world's largest snowman—42 feet tall—greets visitors at a winter festival in Schaumburg, Illinois.

WHO ELSE WAS BORN IN FEBRUARY?
BABE RUTH (George Herman Ruth)

U.S. baseball player
Nicknamed the Bambino, he held over 50 records
when he retired.
BORN February 6, 1895, in Baltimore, Maryland

SUNDAY
February 9

National New Idea Week • In Arlington,
Virginia, 5 inventors are inducted into the
National Inventors Hall of Fame.

MONDAY
February 10

The trial of 474 alleged Mafia criminals begins in Italy.
• 2 twisters tear through Georgia.

TUESDAY
February 11

In Liberal, Kansas, and in Olney, England,
women flip pancakes and run a 415-yard
course in the annual Shrove Tuesday Pancake
Race. The winner: Elizabeth Ann Bartlett
of Olney, by 1.4 seconds.

WEDNESDAY
February 12

Lincoln's birthday • At the Westminster Kennel Club dog
show, Ch. Marjetta National Acclaim, called Deputy, wins
best-in-show out of 2,591 canine contestants.

THURSDAY
February 13

Mudslide alerts throughout California!

FRIDAY
February 14

Valentine's Day • Now on sale for $600: a chocolate
Monopoly game—with pink raspberry play-money!

SATURDAY
February 15

A hot-air balloon reaches a height of 20,226 feet
in Texas, setting a new world record.

SUNDAY
February 16

National Pencil Week • A poodle named Leo, who was bitten
6 times by a rattlesnake while defending his master, is inducted
into the Texas Veterinary Medical Association's Pet Hall of Fame.

SOME INVENTIONS OF 1986

February 11 is National Inventors Day

The microwave clothes dryer
The electronic singing bird
The space garden
Synthetic skin
The plastic pitchfork
The fiber-optic "glowing" carpet

The gaze-controlled computer
The glass electrolyte
The pigtail hat
The electric door for pets
Milk soda
SonomaVoice

MONDAY
February 17

A new study shows that meteorites found in Antarctica are chemically different from those in other areas. They are also far older—usually about 300,000 years old.

TUESDAY
February 18

The worst storm in decades hits the western U.S. with snow, floods, winds, mudslides, and avalanches. The town of Guerneville, California, is completely covered with water; people are sitting on the rooftops!

WEDNESDAY
February 19

The Soviet Union launches a new space station called *Mir*, which means "peace."

THURSDAY
February 20

With a 3-foot-long sword, Prince Charles cuts the world's largest cake in Austin, Texas, at a celebration of the state's 150th birthday. The 90,000-pound cake is made from 3,026 boxes of cake mix, 93,108 eggs, 10,346 cups of oil, and 38,795 cups of water.

FRIDAY
February 21

Astronomers in Chile report that Halley's comet has suddenly grown brighter and now has 7 tails!

1986 CHINESE YEAR OF THE TIGER
February 9, 1986–January 28, 1987

The ancient Chinese calendar is based on the cycles of the moon. According to legend, Buddha summoned all the animals in the world to him one New Year, promising them a reward. Only 12 obeyed, and he gave them each a year: The Rat arrived first, so he got the first year! The order of the 12-year cycle is: Rat, Ox, Tiger, Hare, Dragon, Snake, Horse, Sheep, Monkey, Rooster, Dog, and Pig. People born under the same "sign" are supposed to share certain character traits.

Tigers are very daring, and they fight for what they believe is right. They can be great rebels; they like taking risks and are usually very lucky. They are also sensitive and generous. Tigers get along well with Horses, Dragons, and Dogs but *not* with Snakes, Monkeys, or Oxen.

The Chinese New Year celebration, called Hsin Mien, begins at the first new moon after the sun enters Aquarius, and it lasts four days!

Some famous Tigers:

Princess Anne of
   Great Britain
Tracy Austin
Ludwig van Beethoven
Tony Bennett
Daniel Boone
Emily Brontë
Mel Brooks
Fidel Castro
Miles Davis, Jr.
Joe DiMaggio
Allen Ginsberg

Elliott Gould
Ron Guidry
Evel Knievel
John Knowles
Dorothy Lamour
Gordon Lightfoot
Henry Cabot Lodge
Guy Lombardo
Rod McKuen
Marilyn Monroe
Moshoeshoe II,
   King of Lesotho

Ogden Nash
Joyce Carol Oates
Lilli Palmer
Richard Rodgers
Kenny Rogers
David O. Selznick
Daryl Strawberry
Joan Sutherland
Dylan Thomas
Stevie Wonder
Natalie Wood

Ludwig van Beethoven

Marilyn Monroe

Emily Brontë

SATURDAY
February 22

Washington's birthday • On this day in 1630, Native Americans introduced popcorn to the colonists.

SUNDAY
February 23

In Hawaii, the volcano Kilauea erupts, shooting lava 1,200 feet into the air.

MONDAY
February 24

Full Moon

Emergency pumps are sucking out water at the rate of 35,000 gallons per minute in California's flooded Napa Valley.

TUESDAY
February 25

Corazon Aquino becomes the first woman president of the Philippines, replacing Ferdinand Marcos.

WEDNESDAY
February 26

America's bake-off at Walt Disney World in Florida is won by Mary Lou Warren of Colorado Springs, Colorado, for her lattice-top apple, nut, and golden raisin pie. Prize: $40,000!

FUN FACT '86

Fish have ears and can hear other fish.

THURSDAY
February 27

The U.S. Postal Service issues a 5-cent stamp to commemorate the 100th anniversary of the birth of Hugo L. Black, a famous Supreme Court justice.

FRIDAY
February 28

110 bushels of raw oysters and 26 gallons of hot oysters are eaten at the Volunteer Fire Department Annual Stag Oyster Eat and Dance in Georgetown, Delaware.

SWEDISH PRIME MINISTER ASSASSINATED

PHILIPPINES PRESIDENT MARCOS OUSTED

RUSSIAN FISHERMAN RESCUED FROM FLOATING ICE

TOKYO STUDENT WINS HOT DOG-EATING CONTEST

March

Manch is named for the Roman god of war, Mars.

BIRTHSTONE *Aquamarine*

SATURDAY
March 1

5,000 people set off from Los Angeles, California, on a 9-month, 3,235-mile "peace walk" to Washington, D.C., as a protest against nuclear weapons.

SUNDAY
March 2

The U.S. Postal Service issues a 22-cent stamp to commemorate the 150th anniversary of the day Texas declared its independence from Mexico.

MONDAY
March 3

National Anthem Day • On this day in 1845, Florida became the 27th state of the U.S.

TUESDAY
March 4

A company in Tallahassee, Florida, that has been selling burials in outer space is charged with operating a cemetery without a license!

WEDNESDAY
March 5

DISASTER! Major avalanche in Oslo, Norway.

THURSDAY
March 6

Soviet spacecraft *Vega 1* enters the atmosphere of Halley's comet and sends back pictures of its icy core, which is about 3 miles wide.

FRIDAY
March 7

clean my room? I'll do it later...

This week is National Procrastination Week. • TWA flight attendants go on strike.

SATURDAY
March 8

From the northernmost tip of Canada, a team of explorers headed by Will Steger start for the North Pole. They will make the trip using only dogs and sleds.

SUNDAY
March 9

Soviet spacecraft *Vega 2* flies within 4,990 miles of Halley's comet (closer than *Vega 1*) and sends back proof that the comet's core is solid. Unfortunately, 2 other experiments are ruined by dust particles and space debris!

MONDAY
March 10

MULTIPLE TWISTERS 28 tornadoes rip through Indiana, Ohio, and Kentucky.

WHO ELSE WAS BORN IN MARCH?
GLORIA STEINEM

U.S. feminist, writer, lecturer
She is the founder of the Women's Political Caucus
and the Women's Action Alliance.
BORN March 25, 1934, in Toledo, Ohio

TUESDAY
March 11

Johnny Appleseed Day • 7-year-old Cindy Bergman of Stamford, Connecticut, has won Hallmark's Reading Is Fundamental poster contest. The winning picture: Cindy's mom reading in the tub!

WEDNESDAY
March 12

Girl Scout Day • Popsicle Industries announces that the 2-stick popsicle will be replaced by a new, 1-stick popsicle.

THURSDAY
March 13

The Iditarod sled-dog race in Alaska is won by Susan Butcher, the 2d woman ever to win the Anchorage to Nome race. She also sets a speed record: 11 days, 15 hours, 6 minutes.

FRIDAY
March 14

Giotto, the European Space Agency probe, comes within 335 miles of Halley's comet, the closest any spacecraft has ever been to a comet.

SATURDAY
March 15

An Australian ship rescues 30 Australian scientists who were stranded in Antarctica.

SUNDAY
March 16

A huge lemon known as the American Wonder Lemon has been grown in England. It weighs almost 5 pounds and is about 24 inches in circumference.

THE ELEPHANT WHO WENT ON A DIET

By March 1986, Bunny, the elephant who lives at Mesker Park Zoo in Evansville, Indiana, has lost 640 pounds. For 3 years, she has had low-calorie hay, fewer peanuts, and no monkey biscuits. She's also been exercising: She's been running laps and doing push-ups and deep-knee bends. Now Bunny weighs only 7,200 pounds!

MONDAY
March 17

St. Patrick's Day. 182 U.S. cities hold parades.
• At Yellowstone National Park, the grizzly bears are waking up from their winter sleep; 2 have been seen so far!

TUESDAY
March 18

INSECT NEWS: Experts predict that there will be too many grasshoppers in the U.S. this spring.

WEDNESDAY
March 19

In Muskegon, Michigan, a mysterious man stands on a street corner and hands out 5- and 10-dollar bills to people passing by.

THURSDAY
March 20

Spring equinox • 11-year-old Katerina Lycheva arrives in Chicago from the Soviet Union. To help promote world peace, she has brought paper peace doves made by Russian schoolchildren.

HAPPY 150th!

Texas became an independent territory on March 2, 1836.

State Flower: bluebonnet
State Bird: mockingbird
State Motto: friendship
State Dish: chili
State Tree: pecan
Nickname: the Lone Star State

FRIDAY
March 21

18-year-old Debi Thomas of the U.S. wins the world figure-skating competition in Geneva, Switzerland.

SATURDAY
March 22

National Goof-Off Day • The Weird Beard contest is held at a festival in Vizcaya, Florida.

SUNDAY
March 23

The roof of a swimming club in Laurel, New Jersey, collapses into the pool.

MONDAY
March 24

Scientists in Antarctica have discovered more than 350 fossils that are 225,000,000-years-old, 400 miles from the South Pole.

FUN FACT '86

Elephants talk to one another using sounds that come from their foreheads.

TUESDAY
March 25

The mysterious man in Muskegon, Michigan, who has been giving away money, enters a supermarket and pays for the groceries of 2 lucky shoppers!

WEDNESDAY
March 26

Major forest fires in Virginia, Tennessee, Kentucky, and Ohio. Approximately 3,000 acres are burning.

Full Moon

THURSDAY
March 27

For the first time in 10 years, the volcano Mount Augustine in Alaska erupts, sending a cloud of ash 5 miles into the sky.

FRIDAY
March 28

CABBAGE PATCH SNATCH: 2 people jump out of a car and grab Cabbage Patch dolls from a 6-year-old girl in Wilmington, Delaware. The "doll-nappers" are arrested and the dolls are returned.

SATURDAY
March 29

Sleepy, an epileptic seal who was rescued in February near New Jersey, is being driven to his new home at Sea World in Orlando, Florida.

SUNDAY
March 30

Easter • This year, 250,000 tons of Easter candy has been bought in the U.S. • The NCAA women's basketball championship is won by Texas, which defeats U.S.C., 97–81.

MONDAY
March 31

Mount Augustine, in Alaska, explodes again, shooting ash 8 miles high and blotting out the sun in the nearby town of Homer. • University of Louisville beats Duke in the NCAA men's basketball championship, 72–69.

PESTICIDES FOUND IN MILK

JAPANESE SPACECRAFT STUDY SOLAR WIND

55 TORNADOES SWEEP THE U.S.

CANADA TO REPLACE $1 BILLS WITH $1 COINS

April

*T*he name April comes from the Latin *aperire*, which means "to open." April is known as the time of budding.

BIRTHSTONE *Diamond*

TUESDAY
April 1

April Fools' Day. Radio stations all over the country trick listeners into going to parades that don't exist!

WEDNESDAY
April 2

Rare 12th-century Chinese manuscripts are found inside a Buddhist sculpture at the New Orleans Museum of Art in Louisiana. Experts believe they've been hidden in the sculpture for 800 years.

THURSDAY
April 3

2 French sailors arrive in Miami, Florida, after crossing the Atlantic Ocean on a specially equipped sailboard in 24 days.

FRIDAY
April 4

10 Soviet spacemen begin an experiment to find out what a *very* long space flight would be like. For a year, they will remain flat on their backs with their feet raised.

SATURDAY
April 5

Sleepy, the seal with epilepsy, is settling into his new home at Sea World in Orlando, Florida. His name has been changed to Barney.

SUNDAY
April 6

A group of New Yorkers go up 35,000 feet in a jet and fly over the Atlantic Ocean to get a closer view of Halley's comet.

MONDAY
April 7

CHESS WHIZ: 9-year-old Judith Polgar from Hungary beats all her adult opponents and wins in her section in the New York Open Chess Tournament.

TUESDAY
April 8

Hollywood actor Clint Eastwood, well-known for playing tough guys in movies, is elected mayor of Carmel-by-the-Sea in California.

FUN FACT '86

43,000,000 tons of dust settle on the U.S. every year.

WHO ELSE WAS BORN IN APRIL?
WILLIAM SHAKESPEARE

British playwright and poet
He is thought by many to be the greatest
writer in the English language.
BORN April 26, 1564, in Stratford-upon-Avon,
England

WEDNESDAY
April 9

BEAGLE CALL: The Lyric Opera of Kansas City, Missouri, holds dog auditions to find 6 alert beagles—who won't try to sing with the sopranos! They'll each get $3 a day.

THURSDAY
April 10

Halley's comet comes closest to the earth—only 39,000,000 miles away—today at 4:44 P.M. (EST).
• In Nevada, 96 members of Greenpeace are arrested during a protest against underground nuclear testing.

FRIDAY
April 11

Dodge Morgan arrives in Bermuda, completing a record-breaking solo, nonstop, around-the-world trip in his 60-foot sloop, *American Promise*. The 27,000-mile sail took 150 days.

SATURDAY
April 12

South African Anton Nel wins 7 prizes in the annual Joanna Hodges Piano Conference and Competition in Palm Beach, California.

SUNDAY
April 13

46-year-old Jack Nicklaus wins the Masters golf championship in Augusta, Georgia, for a record 6th time. He is also the oldest person who has ever won the Masters.

MONDAY
April 14

Huge hailstones, weighing as much as 2¼ pounds each, fall in Bangladesh.

TUESDAY
April 15

The first underwater map—complete with underwater volcanoes and earthquake faults—of the sea floor off California, Oregon, and Washington has been released by the U.S. Geological Survey.

WEDNESDAY
April 16

National Gripers' Day • Mount St. Helens spews a 25,000-foot-high fountain of volcanic ash, steam, and gas into the sky.

THURSDAY
April 17

Due to flooding, the Great Salt Lake in Utah is at its highest level since 1876!

FRIDAY
April 18

A Titan 34-D rocket carrying a secret military satellite blows up 5 minutes after lifting off from Vandenberg Air Force Base in California.

SATURDAY
April 19

Scientists, philosophers, and artists meet in Boulder, Colorado, to explore the idea that the planet earth is a living being.
• 2 tornadoes touch down in Texas.

SUNDAY
April 20

National Bike Safety Week • In London, England, 18,336 people run in the 6th London Marathon.

MONDAY
April 21

Rob de Castella of Australia wins the Boston Marathon in a record 2 hours, 7 minutes, 51 seconds. The women's winner: Norway's Ingrid Kristiansen (2 hours, 24 minutes, 55 seconds).

1986 AWARDS BOARD

Nobel Peace Prize: Elie Wiesel
National Teacher of the Year: Guy Doud
National Spelling Bee Champion: Jon Pennington
National Junior Fire Marshall Gold Medal: Paul Bryant
Male Athlete of the Year: Larry Bird, basketball
Female Athlete of the Year: Martina Navratilova, tennis
Horse of the Year: Lady's Secret
Best Movie (Academy Award): *Platoon*
Best Special Visual Effects (Academy Award): *Aliens*
Grammy Award (album): Paul Simon, *Graceland*
Grammy Award (single): Steve Winwood, "Higher Love"
Best children's book (Newbery Medal): *Sarah, Plain and Tall* by Patricia MacLachlan
Best children's book illustration (Caldecott Medal): *The Polar Express*, written and illustrated by Chris Van Allsburg
World Almanac Top Hero of Young America: Bill Cosby

TUESDAY
April 22

Earth Day • In Las Vegas, Nevada, Joel Bobo wins the Hydra-Maniac Slide-a-thon by sliding down a water slide 675 times (a total of 15 miles) in 79 hours, 51 minutes!

WEDNESDAY
April 23

Passover begins at sundown. • 7 of President Reagan's doodles—in pencil on White House stationery—have been bought for $10,000 in New York City.

THURSDAY
April 24

Full Moon

PARACHUTING WITHOUT A PERMIT: 2 Englishmen, Michael McCarthy and Alisdair Boyd, parachute off the 86th floor of the Empire State Building in New York City.

FRIDAY
April 25

Prince Makhosetive Dlamini, age 18, is crowned King Mswati III of Swaziland. He is the youngest king in the world.

SATURDAY
April 26

In the USSR, the nuclear reactor at Chernobyl explodes, sending radioactive debris all over Europe. It is the worst nuclear disaster in history.

SUNDAY
April 27

A video pirate calling himself Captain Midnight interrupts a broadcast on HBO with a message protesting new cable TV fees.

MONDAY
April 28

The National Science Foundation reports that our galaxy is 25 percent smaller than was thought. The new measurements have been taken by a team of astronomers using advanced geometry.

TUESDAY
April 29

Happy 85th birthday to Emperor Hirohito of Japan. • Vermont and New York vote to leave the Lake Champlain monster alone.

WEDNESDAY
April 30

In Massachusetts, Ashrita Furman somersaults more than 12 miles from Lexington to Boston, breaking the world's record for somersaulting—about 8,800 rolls!

U.S. PLANES BOMB LIBYA

FIRST TEST-TUBE BABY BORN

NEW YORK HOLDS BIRTHDAY BASH FOR GODZILLA

ARCHAEOLOGISTS FIND TOMB IN CHINA

May

*M*ay comes from Maia, who was the Roman goddess of growth, increase, and blossoming.

BIRTHSTONE *Emerald*

THURSDAY
May 1

May Day • A false killer whale is born at Sea Life Park in Honolulu, Hawaii, the first of its kind to be born in captivity.

FRIDAY
May 2

After 56 days of walking, jogging, and skiing over snow and ice, the U.S.-Canadian expedition reaches the North Pole aided only by dogsled, the first explorers to do so since 1901.

we made it.

SATURDAY
May 3

Jockey Willie Shoemaker and a horse named Ferdinand win the Kentucky Derby. • A furniture dealer in New York City pays $1,560,000 for a 200-year-old bureau!

SUNDAY
May 4

NASA ground controllers are forced to destroy an unmanned rocket when it goes out of control just 70 seconds after being launched from Cape Canaveral, Florida.

MONDAY
May 5

Soviet cosmonauts Leonid Kizim and Vladimir Solovyov fly from the *Mir* space station to the *Salyut 7* space station 1,850 miles away.

TUESDAY
May 6

70 angry teenagers meet at City Hall in Northampton, Massachusetts. The town has been talking about banning skateboarding!

WEDNESDAY
May 7

Astronomers have detected a powerful invisible source of gravity beyond the Milky Way.

EXPO 86

A world's fair called Expo 86 opens in Vancouver, Canada, on May 2. 54 nations take part, and Prince Charles and Princess Diana officially open the fair. The theme is transportation. Visitors are whisked through the fair on the high-tech Skytrain!

WHO ELSE WAS BORN IN MAY?
CLINT EASTWOOD

U.S. movie actor
Best known for Westerns and for his role of Dirty Harry. In 1986, he became mayor of Carmel-by-the-Sea in California.
BORN May 31, 1930, in San Francisco, California

THURSDAY
May 8
A tornado hits Edmond, Oklahoma. • President Reagan declares June 2–8 National Fishing Week.

FRIDAY
May 9
The UBS *Switzerland* arrives in Portsmouth, England, winning the Whitbread around-the-world yacht race in record time—2 days ahead of its closest competitor.

SATURDAY
May 10
Native American Day • Watch out, video pirate Captain Midnight! The FBI is getting close to catching the person who interrupted HBO on April 27.

SUNDAY
May 11
Mother's Day • Fred Markham sets a record for human-powered speed on a bicycle at Mono Lake in California: 65.484 miles per hour!

FUN FACT '86

140,000,000 Mother's Day cards are bought in the U.S.

MONDAY
May 12
Limerick Day • A blizzard traps a group of mountain climbers on Mount Hood in Oregon.

TUESDAY
May 13
2 rockets spray colorful chemicals into the earth's upper atmosphere, part of a NASA experiment on the origin of the Solar System.

WEDNESDAY
May 14
The *Pride of Baltimore,* one of the tall ships that was to sail into New York Harbor for the July 4th celebration, is hit by a tornadolike wind near Puerto Rico and sinks.

THURSDAY
May 15
Tango, a dog from Port Townsend, Washington, receives the Ken-L Ration Dog Hero of the Year Award in Seattle. He saved his master from an attacking cow.

CIRCUS WEDDING BELLS

On May 2, right before the 1:30 P.M. performance of the Ringling Brothers Barnum & Bailey Circus at Madison Square Garden in New York City, 2 members of the circus get married! The wedding of dancer Laura Litts and clown Jon Weiss takes place in the center ring of the big circus tent. The ceremony includes a ring-bearing bear, 3 four-ton elephant bridesmaids, 12 dancers, and 26 clowns.

FRIDAY
May 16

OPERATION RESCUE: A U.S. Navy pilot has reported seeing a huge SOS written in the sand of a tiny, uninhabited island 300 miles south of Guam!

SATURDAY
May 17

A horse named Snow Chief, ridden by Alex Solis, wins the Preakness in Maryland. • 13-year-old Brian Ewald from Deerfield Beach, Florida, wins the 1986 Mathcounts competition in Washington, D.C.

SUNDAY
May 18

2 people parachute 841 feet off the U.S. Steel Building in Pittsburgh, Pennsylvania. • The longest breakfast table in the world—2,500 feet-long—is set in Springfield, Massachusetts, breaking the previous record of 2,000 feet.

MONDAY
May 19

Anniversary of Dark Day in New England; on this day in 1780, much of New England became almost completely dark. Nobody knows why!

TUESDAY
May 20

Sharon Wood from Canada becomes the first North American woman to climb Mount Everest in the Himalayas.

WEDNESDAY
May 21

A new version of the Soviet *Soyuz* spacecraft, called *Soyuz TM*, is launched; it docks automatically with the space station *Mir*.

THURSDAY
May 22

The first international stamp exhibition in the U.S.— AMERIPEX '86—opens in Chicago, Illinois. About 164,000 people attend.

FRIDAY
May 23

Full Moon

The New China News Agency reports that a rare South China tiger, whose species is almost extinct, has been spotted in the province of Hunan.

SATURDAY
May 24

The Montreal Canadiens win hockey's Stanley Cup championship, defeating the Calgary Flames, 4 games to 1.

SUNDAY
May 25

HANDS ACROSS AMERICA: More than 5,000,000 people join hands to form a line across the U.S., in an effort to raise money for the poor. The 4,150-mile-long human chain is broken only in a few desert areas.

MONDAY
May 26

Memorial Day • Los Angeles car designer Jay Ohrberg has constructed a 60-foot-long Cadillac that has a built-in swimming pool, microwave oven, and satellite dish!

TUESDAY
May 27

The National Research Council of Canada discovers that the figure they have been using for the speed of sound for the past 40 years is incorrect—due to a mistake made in 1942.

WEDNESDAY
May 28

Treasure hunter Mel Fisher brings up 2,300 emeralds from a sunken 17th-century ship, the *Atocha*.

THURSDAY
May 29

14-year-old Jon Pennington from Shiremanstown, Pennsylvania, wins the National Spelling Bee in Washington, D.C. Winning word: *odontalgia* ("toothache").

FRIDAY
May 30

The 3d Great Airplane Toss in Minneapolis, Minnesota, is won by Todd Schlegel.

SATURDAY
May 31

Soviet cosmonauts Leonid Kizim and Vladimir Solovyov walk in space for 4 hours. • Bobby Rahal wins the Indianapolis 500, setting a speed record of 170.7 miles per hour.

FLORIDA DENTIST STRAIGHTENS CAT'S TEETH

SUPERNOVA DISCOVERED BY AMATEUR ASTRONOMER

POCKET WATCH SOLD FOR $1,038,889

JAPAN INTRODUCES DISPOSABLE CAMERA

June

*J*une is named for the Latin *juniores,* meaning "youths," or from the goddess Juno.

BIRTHSTONE *Pearl*

SUNDAY
June 1

In Montana, a snowdrift 6-miles-long and up to 40-feet-deep is blocking the Beartooth Highway; people from Red Lodge—including the mayor in a tuxedo—try to shovel the snow!

MONDAY
June 2

National Fishing Week • William O. Stephens catches a 98-pound flathead catfish in Lewisville, Texas, setting a new world record.

TUESDAY
June 3

About 20,000 Pet Passports have been sold since last December. The passports include space for the pet's photo, medical information, and dietary needs.

WEDNESDAY
June 4

In Baltimore, Maryland, ex-Navy intelligence analyst Jonathan Jay Pollard pleads guilty to charges of spying for Israel.

THURSDAY
June 5

Ross Nathan Power unveils a stainless steel sculpture in his underwater art gallery near Key Largo, Florida. It can be seen only by divers or people in glass-bottom boats.

FRIDAY
June 6

The Vermont Teddy Bear Company announces it is building the world's largest teddy bear (23-feet-tall, weighing 1,200 pounds).

SATURDAY
June 7

The Belmont Stakes is won by a horse named Danzig Connection, ridden by jockey Chris McCarron. • 3 couples get married at the top of a roller coaster in Largo, Maryland.

SUNDAY
June 8

The Boston Celtics win their 16th NBA basketball championship, beating the Houston Rockets, 4 games to 1.

WHO ELSE WAS BORN IN JUNE?
HARRIET BEECHER STOWE

U.S. novelist
She is best known as the author of *Uncle Tom's Cabin*, published in 1852.
BORN June 14, 1811, in Litchfield, Connecticut.

MONDAY
June 9

National Little League Baseball Week begins.
• Happy birthday, Donald Duck!

TUESDAY
June 10

A 7-foot-tall fiberglass statue of Ronald McDonald has been stolen from a McDonald's in Toms River, New Jersey. A ransom note demands 8,891 Chicken McNuggets—with sauce!

WEDNESDAY
June 11

At the Oklahoma City Zoo in Oklahoma, a secretary bird has been hatched—the first in the U.S.

THURSDAY
June 12

The Audubon Park Zoo in New Orleans, Louisiana, introduces the rare Chinese pangolins, which are scaly members of the anteater family. They are the only such animals exhibited in the Western Hemisphere.

FRIDAY
June 13

It's Friday the 13th! Every year has at least one Friday the 13th, but never more than 3. 1986 has just one.

SATURDAY
June 14

National Flag Day • A small replica of Australia's Great Barrier Reef opens at the San Antonio Zoo in Texas. It includes 5 aquariums that hold 85,000 gallons of salt water.

SUNDAY
June 15

Father's Day • Mario Andretti wins the Portland Zoo Auto Race, beating his son by .07 second, the closest finish ever for this race.

MONDAY
June 16

Millions of blacks in South Africa go on strike to protest the government's unfair treatment of them.

TUESDAY
June 17

President Reagan announces that the 78-year-old chief justice of the Supreme Court, Warren E. Burger, is retiring. • Musician Stevie Wonder begins a 60-city tour in Seattle, Washington.

TOP TEN SINGLES OF 1986*

1. "That's What Friends Are For" — Dionne & Friends
2. "How Will I Know" — Whitney Houston
3. "Kyrie" — Mr. Mister
4. "Sara" — Starship
5. "These Dreams" — Heart
6. "Rock Me, Amadeus" — Falco
7. "Kiss" — Prince & the Revolution
8. "Addicted to Love" — Robert Palmer
9. "West End Girls" — Pet Shop Boys
10. "Greatest Love of All" — Whitney Houston

*Source: Billboard.

WEDNESDAY
June 18

The U.S. House of Representatives votes to cut off investments in South Africa because of the country's unfair policies toward blacks.

THURSDAY
June 19

A 30-foot-tall mechanical King Kong is unveiled at Universal Studio Tours in California. • Superstar Michael Jackson has asked for a permit to keep a pet giraffe at his home in Encino, California!

FRIDAY
June 20

It's the 100th day in space for Soviet cosmonauts Leonid Kizim and Vladimir Solovyov, who are aboard orbiting space station *Salyut 7*.

SATURDAY
June 21

Summer solstice • In celebration of the beginning of summer, people in Fairbanks, Alaska, play baseball outside at 11:00 P.M. without using any lights. The day is so long that no lights are necessary.

SUNDAY
June 22

Full Moon

A pair of Mr. Spock's ears are sold for $3,050 at the *Star Trek* convention in Anaheim, California.

MONDAY
June 23

Fifty 7-to 14-year-olds from 16 states compete in the 63d National Marbles Tournament in Wildwood, New Jersey.

TUESDAY *June 24*	**SHIP DELAYED**: It's too windy for the *Virgin Atlantic Challenger II* ocean liner to set off from the Ambrose Light in New York to try to break the transatlantic speed record.
WEDNESDAY *June 25*	Norway's tall ship, *Christian Radich*, arrives in New York Harbor. It's the first of 270 ships expected for the Independence Day–Statue of Liberty weekend.

FUN FACT '86

The fastest swimmer in the world is the cosmopolitan sailfish, which can go 68 miles per hour!

THURSDAY *June 26*	Daredevil Daniel Goodwin of California climbs up the side of the 1,815-foot-high CN Tower in Toronto, Canada—without using safety equipment!
FRIDAY *June 27*	**AUCTION RECORD**: In Reno, Nevada, Jerry Moore buys a rare 1931 Bugatti Royale car for $6,500,000.
SATURDAY *June 28*	Jeff "the Faucet Man" Barber wins the National Tobacco-spitting Contest in Raleigh, Mississippi, with a distance of 33 feet.
SUNDAY *June 29*	The *Virgin Atlantic Challenger II* breaks the transatlantic speed record. The ship crossed the Atlantic Ocean in only 3 days, 8 hours, and 31 minutes.
MONDAY *June 30*	The U.S. Postal Service issues a 14-cent stamp to honor writer Margaret Mitchell. Her best-selling novel, *Gone with the Wind*, was published 50 years ago today.

IDENTICAL TWINS REUNITED AFTER 69 YEARS

FORMER FBI AGENT CONVICTED OF SPYING

IOWA MAN BECOMES NATIONAL GROCERY SACK CHAMP

MOTHER SAVES KIDS FROM PET LION

July

*T*his month was named to honor Julius Caesar.

BIRTHSTONE *Ruby*

TUESDAY
July 1

A Disney cookbook, *Cooking with Mickey Around Our World,* goes on sale today. • Garbage workers go on strike in Philadelphia, Pennsylvania.

WEDNESDAY
July 2

Marine experts have discovered a new type of blind shrimp and a strange 6-sided animal living 2 miles beneath the ocean's surface, 1,800 miles east of Miami, Florida.

THURSDAY
July 3

President Reagan, using a laser beam, lights the new torch of the Statue of Liberty to kick off the 4-day Liberty Weekend celebration in New York City. • 38,000 new U.S. citizens are sworn in.

FRIDAY
July 4

Independence Day. 6,000,000 people crowd the shores of New York Harbor to watch the greatest fireworks display in history: In 28 minutes, 40,000 fireworks shells are launched from 32 barges!

SATURDAY
July 5

For the 5th straight year, Martina Navratilova wins the women's singles title at the Wimbledon tennis tournament. • The International Cherry Pit Spitting contest is held in Eau Claire, Michigan.

SUNDAY
July 6

18-year-old Boris Becker defeats Ivan Lendl and wins the men's singles title at the Wimbledon tennis tournament.

MONDAY
July 7

According to the World Population Institute, there are 5 billion people in the world as of today!

TUESDAY
July 8

6.0
An earthquake measuring 6.0 on the Richter scale rocks Southern California.

WEDNESDAY
July 9

Deep-sea divers set off from Woods Hole, Massachusetts, to explore the wreck of the *Titanic,* which in 1985 was found at the bottom of the sea near Newfoundland, Canada.

WHO ELSE WAS BORN IN JULY?
LOUIS ARMSTRONG

U.S. musician
Nicknamed Satchmo, he is the most famous
trumpet player in jazz history and made over
1,500 recordings.
BORN July 4, 1900, in New Orleans, Louisiana

THURSDAY
July 10

An 18th-century wooden weather vane is sold for a record-breaking price of $121,000 in Portland, Maine.

FRIDAY
July 11

In Dallas, Texas, a 1.92-inch-long cockroach—caught by telephone company employees—wins the Largest-Cockroach Contest.

SATURDAY
July 12

Officials in Paris, France, have approved the plans for EuroDisneyland, which will be 20 miles outside Paris and will cost $1.5 billion.

SUNDAY
July 13

HEAT WAVE: Record high temperatures are reported throughout the Southeast. For the 7th straight day in Columbia, South Carolina, it's over 100 degrees Fahrenheit!

MONDAY
July 14

Dr. Robert Ballard and 2 pilots descend 13,000 feet in a submarine and land on the bridge of the *Titanic,* which sank in 1912.

TUESDAY
July 15

An underwater robot, Jason Jr., enters the *Titanic* through a skylight and travels down a stairway to take pictures of the interior.

FUN FACT '86

The Statue of Liberty weighs as much as 45 large elephants.

WEDNESDAY
July 16

Soviet cosmonauts Leonid Kizim and Vladimir Solovyov return to earth after 125 days in space.

THURSDAY
July 17

In a secret location in Montana, researchers are digging up 70,000,000-year-old dinosaur eggs and other fossils to try to prove that dinosaurs were more like birds than like reptiles.

FRIDAY
July 18

Los Angeles is declared the kazoo capital of the world. • Twin gorillas Moshuba and Macambo fly from Omaha, Nebraska, to the Columbus Zoo in Ohio to visit their father for the summer.

SATURDAY
July 19

Garbage workers are still on strike in Philadelphia, Pennsylvania. More than 33,000 tons of garbage have piled up!

SUNDAY
July 20

In Japan, 99-year-old Teiichi Igarashi climbs Mount Fuji, which is 12,388 feet high, becoming the oldest mountain climber in the world.

MONDAY
July 21
Full Moon

The 4th earthquake in California in 2 weeks shakes parts of California, Nevada, and Utah. The epicenter is 12 miles north of Palm Springs.

HAPPY BIRTHDAY, LADY LIBERTY

On July 4, America celebrates the 100th birthday of the Statue of Liberty. President Reagan starts 4 days of festivities on July 3 by sending a laser beam half a mile across New York Harbor to switch on the colored lights and the statue's torch. The harbor is jammed with 40,000 boats—including 33 naval vessels and 22 tall ships—and about 6,000,000 people, who watch the largest fireworks display in history. The grand finale, on July 6, features the world's largest marching band, 1,000 tap dancers, 5,000 homing pigeons, 75 Elvis Presley imitators, and a 12-story man-made waterfall!

In preparation for the celebration, the statue has undergone a 2-year, $75,000,000 make-over. She has had her nose rebuilt and a spot on her eye removed. The spikes on her crown have been repaired, and her torch has a new gold-leaf flame. She's been strengthened and cleaned inside and out, and there's a new viewing platform with bigger windows inside her crown. But the message written on her base remains the same:

"Give me your tired, your poor,
Your huddled masses yearning to breathe free,
The wretched refuse of your teeming shore
Send these, the homeless, tempest-tost to me.
I lift my lamp beside the golden door!"

TUESDAY
July 22

Captain Midnight surrenders! The video pirate who interrupted HBO's signal in April receives a $5,000 fine and a year's probation.

WEDNESDAY
July 23

ROYAL WEDDING: Prince Andrew marries Sarah Ferguson at 11:30 A.M. in Westminster Abbey in England. The wedding cake is 5½ feet high!

THURSDAY
July 24

The Great Texas Mosquito Festival in Clute, Texas, features a 50-foot inflatable mosquito named Willie Manchew as well as the annual Ms. Quito Beauty Pageant.

FRIDAY
July 25

CONGRATULATIONS! A rare golden monkey has been born at Washington Park Zoo in Portland, Oregon.

SATURDAY
July 26

20,000 cat lovers attend the International Cat Show in Anaheim, California.

SUNDAY
July 27

Greg LeMond becomes the first American to win the 2,500-mile Tour de France bicycle race. Time: 110 hours, 35 minutes, 19 seconds.

MONDAY
July 28

A strong wind blows a train filled with Oreo cookies, shampoo, and skis off a 185-foot-high bridge into the Des Moines River in Boone, Iowa.

TUESDAY
July 29

TIGER ALERT: A white Bengal tiger is loose in the woods near Nicholson, Pennsylvania.

WEDNESDAY
July 30

Another earthquake hits Southern California—this one is only 4.1 on the Richter scale.

THURSDAY
July 31

A fire fighter in Portland, Oregon, rescues 5 kittens from a burning building. He thought their mewing was a baby's crying!

PARIS BOMBED BY TERRORISTS

ROCHESTER, NY WATER POLLUTED BY CATERPILLARS

80,000,000-YEAR-OLD LIZARD FOUND IN TEXAS

30 NATIONS BOYCOTT COMMONWEALTH GAMES

August

August was named in honor of Roman emperor Augustus, whose lucky month it was.

FRIDAY
August 1

The nation's 100 top balloonists lift off from Indianola, Iowa, for the U.S. National Balloon Championships.

SATURDAY
August 2

NEW ZOO: The Burnet Park Zoo opens in Syracuse, New York. The 36-acre park traces the evolution of the earth's inhabitants.

SUNDAY
August 3

In Oregon, 58,000 acres of forest and grassland are burning. The fires were started by at least 1,000 lightning bolts!

MONDAY
August 4

LION HUNT CALLED OFF: A mysterious lion spotted in Waukegan, Illinois, turns out to be just a shaggy dog shaved to look like a lion.

TUESDAY
August 5

Christine Wilson, an astronomy student at the California Institute of Technology, discovers a new comet; Comet Wilson may be as big as Halley's comet.

WEDNESDAY
August 6

A 16-foot, 9-inch-long great white shark is caught off Montauk, Long Island, by Donnie Braddick. It's the largest shark ever caught with a rod and reel.

THURSDAY
August 7

A rare tornado rips through Providence, Rhode Island, wrecking buildings.

FRIDAY
August 8

WORLD'S LARGEST PAJAMA PARTY: In Manchester, Tennessee, the townspeople go to the town square in their pj's and take part in pillow fights, pie fights, piggyback races, and Hula-hooping and pizza-eating contests.

WHO ELSE WAS BORN IN AUGUST?
ORVILLE WRIGHT

U.S. inventor
With his brother, Wilbur, he made the first airplane flight in history on December 17, 1903.
BORN August 19, 1871, in Dayton, Ohio

SATURDAY
August 9

1,700 contestants compete in the 51st annual Old-Time Fiddlers' Convention in Galax, Virginia. Jimmy Edmonds wins first place for all-around performer and for bluegrass fiddle.

SUNDAY
August 10

A giant panda is born in China, a major step in saving the species from extinction.

MONDAY
August 11

Meteor Shower!

The HMS *de Braak*, which sank 2 miles off Delaware in 1798, is raised from the ocean floor.

TUESDAY
August 12

Mexico's president, Miguel de la Madrid Hurtado, arrives for a 3-day visit to the U.S.

WEDNESDAY
August 13

 UFOs? Strange white, red, and green lights in the skies over the eastern U.S. baffle astronomers.

THURSDAY
August 14

79-year-old Rear Admiral Grace Hopper, the oldest active military officer in the country, retires today. • Chickens and ducks are dressed up for a costume poultry contest at the Kentucky State Fair.

FRIDAY
August 15

3 fishermen are rescued off the coast near San Diego, California. They have been clinging to the wreckage of their wooden boat for 13 hours!

SATURDAY
August 16

250 finalists compete in the *Games* magazine/Merriam-Webster 5th annual U.S. Open Crossword Puzzle Championships. Grand prize: $1,500 and a 6-foot pencil.

SUNDAY
August 17

14-year-old Donna Klett wins the 1986 American Publishing National Jigsaw Puzzle Championships in Athens, Ohio, by completing a 500-piece puzzle in 1 hour, 49 minutes, 28 seconds.

MONDAY
August 18

In Conklin, New York, Pamela Hoover saves an injured crow by giving it mouth-to-mouth resuscitation.

TUESDAY
August 19
Full Moon

National Aviation Day • Hurricane Charley, which struck North Carolina 2 days ago, is on its way up the coast.

WEDNESDAY
August 20

Alfred Cawthorne III, a 16-year-old from Quincy, Massachusetts, wins the Space-Science Involvement Program Competition in Cape Canaveral, Florida. His project: to study the effects of low gravity on tadpoles in space.

WHAT'S HOT IN 1986

The Statue of Liberty
Skateboarding
Dinosaurs
Flavored potato chips
Window shades for cars
Teddy bears
Candy rats

Bola ties
Jolt cola
Blizzards (ice cream with candy crumbles)
Biggest-roach contests
Garbage Pail Kids
Rubik's Magic

Scrabble
Fitness
Sportsflics
Muffins
Ferrets
Elephant Polo
White chocolate

THURSDAY
August 21

Texas's biggest cockroach (1.92 inches), which won a Dallas contest on July 11, is presented to the Smithsonian Institution's Insect Zoo in Washington, D.C.

FRIDAY
August 22

A typhoon hits central Taiwan.

SATURDAY
August 23

The New Jersey Championship Tomato Weigh-in is won by Minnie Zaccaria, with an amazing, 4.034-pound tomato.

FUN FACT '86

Prehistoric dragonflies were the size of modern pigeons.

SUNDAY
August 24

In Gulf Breeze, Florida, Jurgen Hergert leaves his glass cage today after spending a record 100 days inside it with 24 poisonous snakes. He wasn't bitten once!

MONDAY
August 25

In England, Geoff Cooper from Wiltshire sets out to row around the world in a 16-foot boat called the *Water Rat*.

TUESDAY
August 26

Teachers' strikes delay the opening of schools in Michigan and Illinois.

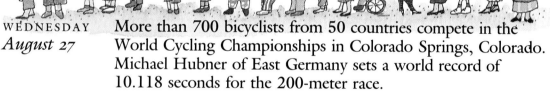

WEDNESDAY
August 27

More than 700 bicyclists from 50 countries compete in the World Cycling Championships in Colorado Springs, Colorado. Michael Hubner of East Germany sets a world record of 10.118 seconds for the 200-meter race.

THURSDAY
August 28

In New York City, the first guitar ever owned by ex-Beatle George Harrison is sold for $6,000.

FRIDAY
August 29

Geoff Cooper, who on Monday set off to row around the world, is rescued after breaking his wrist!

SATURDAY
August 30

A strong earthquake (6.5 on the Richter scale) hits Romania and the Soviet Union, damaging more than 2,300 buildings.

SUNDAY
August 31

In London, England's Chris Bromham breaks his own world record for motorcycle jumping; he leaps 80 yards over 20 trucks.

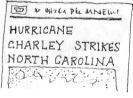

HURRICANE CHARLEY STRIKES NORTH CAROLINA

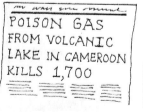

POISON GAS FROM VOLCANIC LAKE IN CAMEROON KILLS 1,700

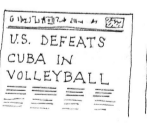

U.S. DEFEATS CUBA IN VOLLEYBALL

U.S. TO SEND WHEAT TO SOVIETS

September

*T*he name September comes from the Latin *septem*, meaning "seven." This was the seventh month of the old Roman calendar.

BIRTHSTONE *Sapphire*

MONDAY
September 1

Labor Day • A Soviet freighter and a cruise ship collide in the Black Sea.

TUESDAY
September 2

3 people in the 15-story-high Dutch hot-air balloon land in a cornfield in Holland and set a new world record for crossing the Atlantic Ocean: 51 hours, 14 minutes.

WEDNESDAY
September 3

HOLE-Y SMOKES: In Potomac, Maryland, golfer Arnold Palmer sets a new world record; he hits a hole in one on the very same hole he hit a hole in one on yesterday!

THURSDAY
September 4

Prince Charles speaks at a celebration for the 350th anniversary of Harvard University in Cambridge, Massachusetts.

FRIDAY
September 5

Be-Late-for-Something Day • The U.S. launches an unmanned rocket on a secret mission to the moon.

TOMATO BATTLE

On September 3d, 600 people in Twin Lakes, Colorado, pelt one another with 7½ tons of ripe tomatoes. The Great Colorado vs. Texas Tomato War has been held every September for 5 years.

SATURDAY
September 6

In Los Angeles, a French doll from the 1880s, nicknamed Long-faced Jumeau, is sold for the record amount of $45,000.

SUNDAY
September 7

Grandparents' Day. Alex Haley, author of *Roots,* is named Grandparent of the Year.

WHO ELSE WAS BORN IN SEPTEMBER?
JESSE OWENS

U.S. athlete
He is remembered for having won 4 gold medals in track and field at the 1936 Olympics in Berlin, Germany.
BORN September 12, 1913, in Danville, Alabama

MONDAY
September 8

Volunteers fly to Alaska to try to save 150 porpoises and seals that are trapped in a lake without food, due to the movement of the Hubbard Glacier.

TUESDAY
September 9

100,000,000-year-old dinosaur tracks have been stolen from private property near Austin, Texas. The tracks, first discovered in 1959, were in limestone bedrock.

WEDNESDAY
September 10

Senator Jake Garn of Utah donates one of his kidneys to his daughter in a transplant operation.

THURSDAY
September 11

On Wall Street, the stock market plunges 86.61 points. • In West Glamorgan, England, Barry Kirk is trying to break the world record for sitting in a bath of cold baked beans.

FRIDAY
September 12

A Coast Guard cargo plane arrives in Yakatat, Alaska, with tons of equipment for the rescue of 150 trapped sea mammals. So far, attempts to airlift them to safety have failed.

SATURDAY
September 13

The National Geographic Society reports the capture of the oldest known hummingbird in North America. The 11-year-old female was caught in Gothic, Colorado.

SUNDAY
September 14

The world's largest apple strudel is baked in Schoharie, New York, in a 40-foot pipe oven. It contains 689 pounds of puff pastry, 879 pounds of apples, and more than 200 pounds of sugar. The strudel is 1,440 feet long!

MONDAY
September 15

800,000 baby bay scallops are flown from Maine to Long Island to help reseed the scallop population.

TUESDAY
September 16

International Day of Peace. U.S. students paint balloons to look like the earth, attach peace messages, and release them into the sky. People all over the world stand in silence for one minute and think about peace.

SCHOOLROOM TRIVIA

In the U.S. in 1986, the number of students for each teacher is the lowest in Wyoming, where there are only about 13½ students per teacher. The highest number of students per teacher is in Utah—with about 24 students for each teacher.

WEDNESDAY
September 17

William Rehnquist is confirmed as the new chief justice of the U.S. Supreme Court.

THURSDAY
September 18
Full Moon

MILK SODA? Researchers of the United Dairy Association have found a way to put bubbles in milk!

FRIDAY
September 19

Philippine president Corazon Aquino addresses 5,000 Peace Corps veterans in Washington, D.C., at a ceremony marking the Peace Corps's 25th anniversary.

SATURDAY
September 20

An electronic door for pets has been invented—it unlocks when a pet wearing a magnetic key comes near it.

SUNDAY
September 21

In Detroit, Michigan, Larry Farmer sets a world record for running backward, winning the quarter-mile Metro Retro race in 1 minute, 16.08 seconds.

MONDAY
September 22

Members of the Great Peace March, which began in Los Angeles on March 1, cross into Ohio. They hope to reach Washington, D.C., by November.

WELCOME TO OHIO

TUESDAY
September 23

 Autumn equinox. Fall begins at exactly 7:59 A.M. (EST). • The House of Representatives votes to make the rose the U.S. national flower.

WEDNESDAY
September 24

Mount Etna erupts in Sicily: A new crack opens in the northeast summit, and a black cloud of volcanic ash floats into the sky.

THURSDAY
September 25

A rare, shiny 1894-S Barber Head dime—one of only a dozen of its kind in the world—is bought for $83,000 in San Francisco.

FRIDAY
September 26

Happy birthday to Baby Shamu, the first killer whale to be born and survive in captivity. She's one year old today and lives at Sea World in Florida.

SATURDAY
September 27

New York City's Bronx Zoo opens a new exhibit called Himalayan Highlands that houses the zoo's 17 snow leopards.

SUNDAY
September 28

Researchers in Nova Scotia, Canada, are digging up evidence they hope will prove there were animals that became extinct 125,000,000 years before dinosaurs did.

FUN FACT '86

 80 percent of the earth's creatures are insects or spiders.

MONDAY
September 29

3 bombs explode in downtown Coeur d'Alene, Idaho. Police are on the alert for more.

TUESDAY
September 30

The Goddard Space Flight Center in Greenbelt, Maryland, reports that rain may be falling from Saturn's rings.

NEW DRUG AZT MAY HELP AIDS PATIENTS

GOLD MINE EXPLOSION IN SOUTH AFRICA

FIRST U.S. GOLD COIN MINTED

KETCHUP MUSEUM OPENS IN PITTSBURGH, PA

October

*O*ctober was the eighth month of the old Roman calendar; the name is from the Latin *octo,* meaning "eight."

BIRTHSTONE *Opal*

WEDNESDAY
October 1

Former U.S. president Jimmy Carter dedicates a new library and museum—the Carter Presidential Center—in Atlanta, Georgia.

THURSDAY
October 2

Happy birthday: Charlie Brown and Snoopy are 36 today, and Walt Disney World is 15!

FRIDAY
October 3

Rosh Hashanah begins at sundown. • Fire breaks out on a Soviet nuclear submarine 600 miles east of Bermuda.

SATURDAY
October 4

The world's rarest clock has been sold to a collector in London for more than $2,000,000. The clock, the Rose, has 9,000 parts and even tells the temperature.

SUNDAY
October 5

New Jersey has decided to make the tomato the state's official vegetable (even though it's a fruit).

MONDAY
October 6

Major floods in the Midwest: Cattle are stranded on top of a roof in Fort Scott, Kansas.

TUESDAY
October 7

At the National Soft Drink Expo in Dallas, Texas, chocolate-chip soda is introduced to the world!

WEDNESDAY
October 8

The porpoises and seals trapped in Russell Lake in Alaska are freed as the Hubbard Glacier ice dam breaks, allowing water to rush out of the lake.

THURSDAY
October 9

For the 2d year in a row, Gary Kasparov beats Anatoly Karpov in the world championship chess match in Leningrad in the Soviet Union.

FRIDAY
October 10

At the National Archives in Washington, D.C., a man with a hammer smashes the glass case that holds original copies of the U.S. Constitution, the Declaration of Independence, and the Bill of Rights. The documents are unharmed.

WHO ELSE WAS BORN IN OCTOBER?
JIMMY CARTER

U.S. statesman
Peanut farmer, nuclear engineer, and the 39th
president of the U.S. (1977–1981).
BORN October 1, 1924 in Plains, Georgia

SATURDAY
October 11

President Reagan and Soviet leader Gorbachev meet in Iceland for arms-control talks.

SUNDAY
October 12

Astronomers say they have found 2 stars that have collided; the stars seem to be spinning around each other every 11 minutes!

MONDAY
October 13

Columbus Day and Yom Kippur • Bob Gancarz wins the Great Pumpkin Weigh-off in Collins, New York, with a record-breaking 671-pound pumpkin.

TUESDAY
October 14

Winnie the Pooh is 60 today. • Elie Wiesel, writer and Holocaust survivor, is named winner of the Nobel Peace Prize.

WEDNESDAY
October 15

A balloon the size of a football field is launched from the National Scientific Balloon Facility in Palestine, Texas. It carries a special telescope whose purpose is to record gamma-ray images.

THURSDAY
October 16

A Soviet research station in Antarctica has vanished. Officials believe a chunk of coastal ice has broken off, carrying the station with it.

FUN FACT '86

There are 50 million cats in the U.S.

FRIDAY
October 17
Full Moon

A bamboo-eating primate called the greater bamboo lemur, which experts had thought was extinct, has been discovered in Madagascar.

PARACHUTING IN 1986

1986 seems to be a year for parachute jumping, even though on October 11, Bridge Day in Fayetteville, West Virginia, only about 40 people parachute off the New River Gorge Bridge while 200,000 spectators watch. High winds keep the other 360 who had planned to jump from taking the plunge! On October 17, parachutist Nicholas Feteris leaps from the Statue of Liberty's torch as about 300 people watch. He is arrested for trespassing.

Other jumps in 1986:

February 5: 89-year-old Edwin Townsend jumps from a plane in Vermillion Bay, Louisiana.

April 24: Englishmen Michael McCarthy and Alisdair Boyd leap off the Empire State Building in New York City.

May 18: 2 people parachute 841 feet from the U.S. Steel Building in Pittsburgh, Pennsylvania.

SATURDAY
October 18
A platinum Boehm system flute is bought for $187,000 in New York City—the most ever paid for a flute.

SUNDAY
October 19
A musician from Los Angeles leads several hundred people in a "Central Park Hum" in New York City; they hum together in a 75-foot-long tunnel in the key of E flat!

MONDAY
October 20
The *Queen Elizabeth II* leaves New York City for Southampton in England, for her last crossing of the Atlantic Ocean before she goes into dry dock.

TUESDAY
October 21
COUGAR HUNT: Rangers in San Juan Capistrano, California, are on the lookout for a dangerous cougar.

WEDNESDAY
October 22
Participants in the Great Peace March, who are walking across the country as a demonstration for peace, enter New York today.

THURSDAY
October 23

San Juan Capistrano, California: No sign of the cougar. The hunt is called off.

FRIDAY
October 24

A British horse named Dancing Brave flies from Gatwick, England, to Los Angeles, where he will spend 28 hours in quarantine before racing in the Breeders' Cup in Santa Anita, California.

SATURDAY
October 25

The largest omelet in the world is made in Las Vegas, Nevada. It contains 54,763 eggs and 531 pounds of cheese, and is cooked in a frying pan 30 feet in diameter.

SUNDAY
October 26

China begins broadcasting Disney cartoons on TV.

MONDAY
October 27

World Peace Day • The New York Mets win baseball's World Series, defeating the Boston Red Sox, 4 games to 3.

TUESDAY
October 28

The Statue of Liberty was unveiled and dedicated on this day 100 years ago.

WEDNESDAY
October 29

At an auction in New York City, a letter written by Thomas Jefferson in 1818 is sold for $360,000—the highest price ever paid for a signed letter.

THURSDAY
October 30

A cat named Pumpkin wins the Magical Musical Meow-off singing contest in New York City. The 6 competing cats are accompanied by an orchestra and 2 singers.

FRIDAY
October 31

Halloween • In New Delhi, India, a snake has closed down an engineering factory. The cobra has been in the owner's office for 2 months and won't get out!

SOVIET NUCLEAR SUB SINKS

SURGEON REPLACES FINGERS WITH TOES

FLOATING PIZZA SEEN IN ILLINOIS

RUBY NECKLACE SOLD FOR $1,540,000

November

*N*ovember was the ninth month of the old Roman calendar.
The name comes from the Latin *novem,* meaning "nine."

BIRTHSTONE *Topaz*

SATURDAY
November 1

About 4,000 people show up at a farm in central Vermont to try to catch a glimpse of a moose that has fallen in love with a cow!

Hi cutie!

SUNDAY
November 2

Gianni Poli from Italy wins the New York Marathon with a time of 2 hours, 11 minutes, 6 seconds. The women's winner is Grete Waitz of Norway (2 hours, 28 minutes, 6 seconds).

MONDAY
November 3

The largest gem-quality uncut black opal in the world is found in Australia. It's 2,020 carats and is named Halley's comet.

TUESDAY
November 4

A frog loses the election for Douglas County commissioner in Kansas. Agnes T. Frog gets 1,850 votes; her human opponent, 4,886.

Bummer!

WEDNESDAY
November 5

Newly found fossils in China suggest that dinosaurs actually died out 1,000,000 years later than experts thought.

THURSDAY
November 6

Cecilia Rubio's lemon meringue pie wins the American Pie Contest in Nashville, Tennessee.

FRIDAY
November 7

An 8-foot-tall fiberglass statue of Superman is dedicated in Metropolis, Illinois.

SATURDAY
November 8

Cleveland, Ohio—inspired by similar contests in other cities— holds a biggest-roach contest. The winner: a 2¼-inch roach found by Jeronica Bell.

SUNDAY
November 9

In Reykjavík Harbor in Iceland, 4 whaling ships are sunk by environmentalists who want to save the whales.

WHO ELSE WAS BORN IN NOVEMBER?
MARIE CURIE

Polish-French chemist and physicist
Famous for her work with radioactivity. She
and her husband Pierre were awarded the Nobel
Prize in physics in 1903; she received the
Nobel Prize in chemistry in 1911.
BORN November 7, 1867, in Warsaw, Poland

MONDAY
November 10

A painting by American artist Jasper Johns called
Out the Window is sold for $3,600,000!

TUESDAY
November 11

Veteran's Day • A team of scientists say that a
huge raindrop about the size of a dime has been
found in a cloud just east of Hawaii.

WEDNESDAY
November 12

Planet 3147, an asteroid between Mars and Jupiter, has
been named for Samantha Smith, the famous 11-year-old
who visited the USSR in 1983 on a peace mission.

THURSDAY
November 13

A satellite is launched from Vandenberg Air Force Base in
California. It will be in polar orbit around the earth and should
improve communications between spacecraft and ground
control.

FRIDAY
November 14

At the Future Farmers of America Convention in
Kansas City, Missouri, Chris Thompson of Midland
City, Alabama, is named Star Farmer of America.

FUN FACT '86
A bat can eat 3,000 bugs a night.

SATURDAY
November 15

Joseph Yates of Barling, Arkansas, wins the $100,000 first
prize in the Red Man All-American Bass Championship at
Lake Havasu in Arizona.

SUNDAY
November 16

On November 16, 1811, an earthquake in Missouri caused
the Mississippi River to flow backward!

Full Moon

MONDAY
November 17

UFO: The crew of a Japan Air Lines 747 cargo jet spots a giant, walnut-shaped object with flickering, yellow-white lights. The mysterious craft, which seems to be traveling with 2 smaller objects, follows the jet for 500 miles over Alaska before disappearing.

TUESDAY
November 18

USA Today reports that a 2-year-old boy who wandered away from home in Keedysville, Maryland, has been found on a country road, with 4 dogs huddled around him to keep him warm!

WEDNESDAY
November 19

The northeastern U.S. is hit by up to 17 inches of snow.

THURSDAY
November 20

Dozens of blue whales—the world's largest living creatures—appear unexpectedly off the coast of Monterey, California. Scientists think they've come for the pink, shrimplike krill, which are the whales' favorite food.

FRIDAY
November 21

On the Japanese island O-shima, a volcano explodes, sending lava streaming toward the largest town. Thousands of people flee.

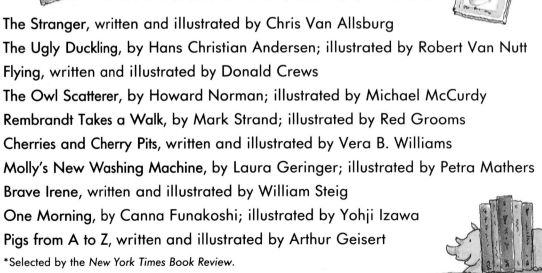

TOP TEN ILLUSTRATED
CHILDREN'S BOOKS OF 1986*

The Stranger, written and illustrated by Chris Van Allsburg

The Ugly Duckling, by Hans Christian Andersen; illustrated by Robert Van Nutt

Flying, written and illustrated by Donald Crews

The Owl Scatterer, by Howard Norman; illustrated by Michael McCurdy

Rembrandt Takes a Walk, by Mark Strand; illustrated by Red Grooms

Cherries and Cherry Pits, written and illustrated by Vera B. Williams

Molly's New Washing Machine, by Laura Geringer; illustrated by Petra Mathers

Brave Irene, written and illustrated by William Steig

One Morning, by Canna Funakoshi; illustrated by Yohji Izawa

Pigs from A to Z, written and illustrated by Arthur Geisert

*Selected by the *New York Times Book Review*.

SATURDAY
November 22

The Santa Express, a diesel train carrying Santa Claus, toys, and candy, chugs through parts of Kentucky, Virginia, and Tennessee—dropping goodies as it goes.

SUNDAY
November 23

In Solon, Ohio, Jeanne Maiden sets a world record for women's highest bowling score: 864 (3 sanctioned games).

MONDAY
November 24

More than 1,000 weekend skiers are stranded on Mount Baker by floods, and 80 families are evacuated from the Snoqualmie, Washington, area.

TUESDAY
November 25

Roads are reopened in Snoqualmie, Washington. Stranded skiers are freed and evacuees return home!

WEDNESDAY
November 26

Nutcracker: The Motion Picture opens in theaters across the country. The sets were designed by children's book author and illustrator Maurice Sendak.

THURSDAY
November 27

 Thanksgiving • White-hot lava from the volcano Kilauea buries 9 homes in Kalapana, Hawaii.

FRIDAY
November 28

So far, nearly 50,000 people have traveled to Shrewsbury, Vermont, to see a moose named Stanley courting a cow named Jessica.

SATURDAY
November 29

Opening day of the World Championship Duck-calling Contest in Stuttgart, Arkansas.

SUNDAY
November 30

Richard Pramotton of Italy wins the men's World Cup giant slalom race in Italy; Switzerland's Corinne Schmidhauser wins the women's World Cup slalom race in Utah.

PRESIDENT REAGAN ADMITS SECRET ARMS DEAL WITH IRAN

McDONALD'S RESTAURANTS TO BE BUILT IN YUGOSLAVIA

2 BIRDS FLY SOUTH FOR WINTER BY PLANE

U.S. AND SOVIETS AGREE TO EXPLORE MARS TOGETHER

December

*D*ecember used to be the tenth month of the year (the Latin *decem* means "ten"). The old Roman calendar began with March.

BIRTHSTONE *Turquoise*

MONDAY
December 1

A survey shows that only 46 percent of America is happy with President Reagan; his popularity plunge is due to the Iran-contra arms scandal.

TUESDAY
December 2

The largest electric sign in the world is lit in Davenport, Iowa. It uses 2,250 spotlights, has letters 7 feet high, and can be seen from 3 miles away!

WEDNESDAY
December 3

Scientists and volunteers in Eastham, Massachusetts, are trying to push 50 beached pilot whales back out to sea.

THURSDAY
December 4

MITTEN DONATION: In Baltimore, Maryland, kids and adults hang mittens, to be given to charity, on the city's Christmas tree.

FRIDAY
December 5

Treasure hunter Mel Fisher sells most of his salvage company, his museum, and some items from the sunken ship *Nuestra Señora de Atocha* for $7,000,000.

SATURDAY
December 6

1,500 people attend the 4-H Club's 65th National 4-H Congress in Chicago, Illinois.

SUNDAY
December 7

Auburn University running back Bo Jackson receives the Heisman Trophy for outstanding college football player of 1985.

MONDAY
December 8

The molten lava from Kilauea is once again flowing into the sea, after having created 20 acres of new land off Hawaii's south coast.

TUESDAY
December 9

American and British researchers announce that the earth's core is not a smooth sphere, as was thought, but has mountains taller than Mount Everest and valleys 6 times deeper than the Grand Canyon!

WHO ELSE WAS BORN IN DECEMBER?
HOWARD HUGHES

U.S. businessman
He was one of the richest men in the world and
became a recluse in his later years.
BORN December 24, 1905, in Houston, Texas

WEDNESDAY
December 10

The redesigned shuttle booster is test-fired successfully in
Brigham City, Utah.

THURSDAY
December 11

The Soviet antarctic research station
missing since October 16 has been found
in the Weddell Sea, floating on an iceberg.

FRIDAY
December 12

National Ding-a-ling Day • The U.S. Postal Service issues a
new stamp in honor of the 350th anniversary of the National
Guard.

SATURDAY
December 13

A 202-year-old bottle of wine once owned by Thomas
Jefferson has been sold in London for $56,628—the most ever
paid for a bottle of white wine.

SUNDAY
December 14

Twin-engine aircraft *Voyager 4* takes off from Edwards Air
Force Base in California, in an attempt to fly nonstop around
the world.

MONDAY
December 15

Happy birthday to the Bill of Rights, the
first 10 amendments to the U.S. Constitution,
which was passed on December 15, 1791.

TUESDAY
December 16

Full Moon

Ronald Pelton, a former National Security Agency employee, is
sentenced to life in prison for selling military secrets to the
Soviets.

WEDNESDAY
December 17

British surgeons perform the world's first triple transplant,
replacing a patient's heart, lungs, and liver.

THURSDAY
December 18

Officials of the U.S. and USSR agree to work together to try
to stop the hole in the ozone layer from getting bigger.

FRIDAY
December 19

Underdog Day • Melanie Feldman sets a new fishing record by catching a 72-pound, 12-ounce tope (a small shark) in New Zealand.

SATURDAY
December 20

In New London, Connecticut, 15-year-old Marie Lago from Mystic becomes the first girl in the state to wrestle on a boy's team.

SUNDAY
December 21

Winter solstice • More than 50,000 Chinese students demonstrate in People's Square in Shanghai for democracy.

MONDAY
December 22

37 oil-rig workers are rescued in the Gulf of Mexico, after abandoning their offshore drill rig because of the danger of an explosion.

FUN FACT '86

By the end of 1986, there are a million millionaires in the U.S.

TUESDAY
December 23

Pilots Dick Rutan and Jeana Yeager land their experimental aircraft, *Voyager 4,* at Edwards Air Force Base in California. They have flown around the world nonstop in a record 9 days, 3 minutes, and 44 seconds, without refueling.

WEDNESDAY
December 24

Christmas Eve • The Carnegie Hero Fund commission honors 24 heroes, including Bradley Hall, who crawled on his stomach 28 feet to drag a disabled man out of a burning house.

THURSDAY
December 25

Christmas • The *New York Times* reports that a 52-year-old woman in Albany, New York, successfully fought off a mugger by hitting him with her hot fudge sundae!

TOY BOX '86

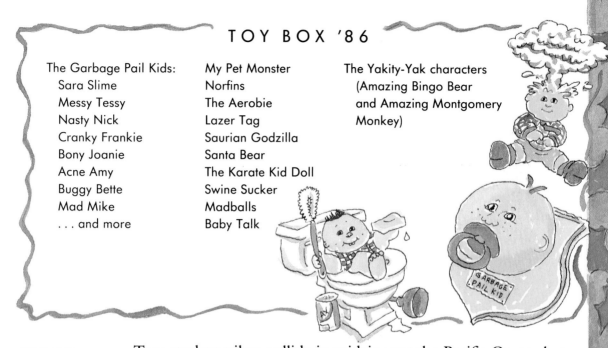

The Garbage Pail Kids:
- Sara Slime
- Messy Tessy
- Nasty Nick
- Cranky Frankie
- Bony Joanie
- Acne Amy
- Buggy Bette
- Mad Mike
- . . . and more

My Pet Monster
Norfins
The Aerobie
Lazer Tag
Saurian Godzilla
Santa Bear
The Karate Kid Doll
Swine Sucker
Madballs
Baby Talk

The Yakity-Yak characters
(Amazing Bingo Bear
and Amazing Montgomery
Monkey)

FRIDAY
December 26

Two student pilots collide in midair over the Pacific Ocean, but manage to land their planes safely.

SATURDAY
December 27

Hanukkah • Museums in Massachusetts are joining together to help save the nearly extinct Plymouth red-bellied turtle.

SUNDAY
December 28

Australia triumphs over Sweden, 3 matches to 2, to win tennis's Davis Cup.

MONDAY
December 29

At a special ceremony in Los Angeles, President Reagan presents Presidential Citizen's medals to Jeana Yeager and Dick Rutan, *Voyager 4*'s pilots.

TUESDAY
December 30

The National Marine Fisheries Service has opened a school for salmon—to teach them how to avoid being eaten by other fish!

WEDNESDAY
December 31

New Year's Eve • Data from the *Solar Max* satellite shows that the sun is growing a little bit dimmer each year.

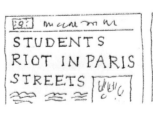

HOTEL FIRE KILLS 96 IN PUERTO RICO

POPE VISITS 6 NATIONS

STUDENTS RIOT IN PARIS STREETS

WOMAN BEATS THIEF WITH ICE CREAM

YOUR YEAR AT A GLANCE

A lot happened the year you were born. How many events shown on the cover can you identify? Turn the page upside down for the answers.

1. There are 50 million cats in the U.S. (See October Fun Fact.) 2. The Statue of Liberty turns 100 (July 4). 3. World's largest snowman greets visitors in Schaumburg, Illinois (February 8). 4. Poultry costume contest takes place at the Kentucky State Fair (August 14). 5. Vermont moose falls in love with a cow (November 1). 6. English man attempts record for sitting in a bath of cold baked beans (September 11). 7. Skateboarding is hot in 1986 (See August). 8. Circus clown and dancer get married in the big top (See May). 9. Three couples wed at top of roller coaster (June 7). 10. Twenty-eight tornadoes rip through Indiana, Ohio, and Kentucky (March 10).